Ghosts & Birthdays

Poems

Red Shuttleworth

Humanitas Media Publishing

Ghosts & Birthdays

Poems

Author Website: http://poetredshuttleworth.blogspot.com

Cover art and author photo by Ciara Shuttleworth.

Published by Humanitas Media Publishing. For all inquiries, please contact us at info@humanitasmedia.com

http://www.humanitasmedia.com

ISBN: 978-0615738284 (Print)

Acknowledgements

A number of the poems in this collection first appeared in the following journals:

Aethlon: "Jack Johnson (1909)"

Blue Mesa Review: "Dwight David Eisenhower (1952)"

Chariton Review: "Henry Starr (1921)" and "Theodore Roosevelt (1904)"

Chiron Review: "Gabby Hayes (1951)" and "Sonny Liston (1970)"

Chattahoochee Review: "Hank Williams (1952/1953)" and "Jinx Falkenburg (1941)"

Concho River Review: "Georgia O'Keefe (1913)"

Elysian Fields Quarterly: "Dante Benedetti (1929)" and "Ted Williams (1972)"

Flyway: "Jack London (1910)"

Interim: "Marilyn Monroe (1960)"

Los Angeles Review: "Going to the Movies with Gertrude Stein"

Roundup Magazine: "Jane Russell (1941)" and "Will Rogers (1935)"

Suisun Valley Review: "Postcard to Kay Boyle" and "Wyatt Earp (1909)"

" Huron "Ted" Walters (1938)" and "Lyndon Baines Johnson (1928)" were first published in *Open Range* (Denver: Ghost Road Press, 2007).

To the Memory
of
Kay Boyle

Contents

Glide Safe Over Every Edge

In deliriums
of love and faith
is there a music
to preserve
gold light…
if only
for seconds…
so we may
eagerly wash
across those we
care most deeply for?

Good Girl, Wind-Girl, Hunger-Girl: Lilith

Exiled from the overstuffed Garden.
Just an eye blink away from the first bus station.

Listen to the wet eyes of the devout:
soda cans rolling in the back of a Greyhound.

Copper lightning. Desert. Moon-sigh.
Turkey vultures dressed in white linen.

Havre to Minot: crystal goblets of oily water,
the lost twitching legs of suicides on railroad tracks.

Forever young-as-brass Lilith takes the ride:
guitar-lace-perfume. Astonished passengers!

Song of tawny fire, ex-husbands Adam and Samael.
God of Emptiness song. Empty of any god song.

Bacterial silence in northern Nevada motel rooms.
The hideous, screaming weight of dying stars.

Badger-stench cosmos, glass planets, ooze planets:
birth-love-death… like a trick off-ramp with quicksand.

Lilith scatters yellow rose petals from a bus window,
sings for any outlaw of the rubble-road of strangers.

Julius Caesar
(July 13, 100 BC – March 15, 44 BC)

Perhaps you are a comet now… providing joy rides
across the cosmos for Jupiter. As a birthday present
to you in 1881, Pat Garrett shot dead one Billy the Kid.
The next July 13th Johnny Ringo shot himself
so that he might address you in his cracked Latin.
Forgotten are Marcus Themus and Servilius Isaricus,
your military mentors. Descent from Venus
weighed heavy enough for you to dirty-fuck
goddess-queen Cleopatra… your son by her
later murdered in Rome upon your dying blood.
Perhaps you are a comet, riotously laughing,
seeking a planet you can crash into:
a final relieving of all the other deities'
silly indulgences and interventions.
Tonight's sky blazes purple.

Catullus Speaks to Clodia Metelli

Here the pleasure and mud-prowl.
We float. Lust-thirst… and drink.
Wolf-runs. Your bared breasts.
Bared teeth. Twitchy-thighed you.
Perfume of rumor. Are you feeling languid?
Is all this a temple to your brassy laughter?

We are the *new people* we are seeing.
All-nighters when your husband shambles
from town to village… selling spliced wire,
foreclosed villas, blackout candles.
We are star-drugged lovers,
restless wind and laughter.
It's only pleasure. You stir morning.

Less sleep. My warrior-poet body thins.
The sheen of my seed on your inner thighs,
on your belly, on breasts, on your lips,
inside your womb, your fists frantic upon my back,
your plum-painted fingernails clawing me closer.
You whisper, *We are innocent… dear friends…*
only desperate friends tending to quirky pain.
Thrust and thrust and thrust atop thrust
through folds of your silk nightgown,
a spear into *a new woman of Now-Now-Now, baby.*
Your granite bed covered with pillows.
You laugh, *This is friendship… the secret gift.*

You have not soothed me, Clodia-Lesbia-Clodia.
Yes, we are a measure *of more than the mortal nothing.*
Your husband shakes my hand at the temple,
asks after my verse, back-slaps me jovially.
You, Clodia-Lesbia-Clodia, smirk,
lower mirthful eyes, toy with your long hair
gathered up with pins and needles.

Nakedness and wild desire-frolics.
You are the same as many others before you.
Let me go. Keep me. Let me go.
When we meet in town, we are strangers.
Radiant beauty of your husband's refusal to see.
Diverted to and from love by your marriage.
The sun-kissed taste of your flesh.

I am leaving you.

Returning right away.

The blue flame in my heart is for you.
I am running alone. You are running alone.
Azure sky. Cracked daylight moon.

Mikhail Lermontov
(October 15, 1814 – July 27. 1841)

Today's poets do not enter pistol duels.
They suck cigarettes, sip wine, pontificate
beneath lush maple trees in university towns.
Today's poets marry their chalk-face kind.
I hear your shade, brother, laugh at so-called men
as they sponge dishes and change toddler diapers
while their fatty princesses gibber to each other.
The knuckles of their fleshy hands are scarless.

Fire ran, no compromise, in your arteries,
Lermontov. Women's faces turned rosy
as you passed, scarcely acknowledging
the probability of warm nights they'd give you.
Horseman-warrior, you sang of honor for the sturdy.

No bitter tears for you tonight.
Yes… the absurdity of depression,
that surprising sadness without reason.
More battle, more whiskey, more poetry!
So much is the confusion of melodrama.
None of that! Bring on the court jesters,
the false poets… bring out the dueling pistols!

Sam Houston

Texas was radiant for grazing.
There was prairie meat.
Clouds grasped him.
An Indian girl scrubbed
rust out of an enormous
iron tub as Houston
fed her canned peaches
with a wooden spoon.
She taught coyote lingo
like a nun translating Horace.

A huge laughing beast,
Houston ordered *his* creation
to peer deep, deep into *his*
razor-sharp eyes.

Blackthorn night,
Gravestone Texas dawn,
he dispatched leather postcards
to Andy Jackson, nicknamed
the lice in his hair *citizen,*
sat a white meat-eating
stallion like a Roman emperor.

Houston bragged,
*My life has the crimson
hue of proof.
No god favors
conformity or caution.*

Georg Buchner
(October 17, 1813 – February 19, 1837)

The panic experiments of medicine are still with us,
every sick man a *Woyzeck*, afraid to piss…
the diets and pills no better than desert-orange dirt.

I ran into your man, *Woyzeck,* in Vegas
a few dodgy years ago, banging his head
off car hoods in a casino parking lot,
his Maria watching from a street corner,
infant in a tiny, damp and smothering stroller.
She sure was a luster… kind of girl
who can make money in a bubble bath
chewing celery stalks and smirking-pretty.

Woyzeck never got to heaven,
never got to help out with the thunder, no.
The cops took away his bloody butcher knife.
Maria screeched scab-brown laughter,
shouted, *So much for your fever-talk.*
Let the captains and kings have at me.

And you, dramatist of the common man,
dead from typhus… worm-plundered at twenty-three.
You guessed right, *Mortal sin can be so beautiful.*
And you got precious little of its juices
before plunging into graveyard mud,
a pauper's shroud around your wasted body.

Fyodor Tyutchev
(December 5, 1803 – July 27, 1873)

Night-flutter of birds in the pines out front,
like the rustle of a young Bavarian widow's skirt
as she sits to read a poem of crystal-blue skies,
tender smiles, love, and death. No mention
of a diplomat's dandruff, nor of grumbles
over another man's wildfire-beloved going cold
after application of a new gold wedding band.
You made glossy-best of Russian winters,
wrote warmer poems in Athens, Rome,
and, best of all, with bunioned feet
at play in Swiss lakes. The snowy, rutted roads
to and from the estate, Ovstug, were depressing,
like a smelly maid's oat-colored quivering buttocks.
The poems cried out to be written, but you scrunched
most of them in your fist, saying, *We all vanish,*
why not my tiny cups of salted watery wine?

Happy Birthday, Billy the Kid
(November 23, 1859 – July 14, 1881)

It'll be in the sixties, sunny skies, later today
near your Fort Sumner, New Mexico, grave…
when tourists' salty tears splat the dry ground.
They saw the movie. Or all the movies.
There's always someone who believes
he bought one of your boots or a tooth.
So much of the past is crippled memory
blackened from bitterness or for profit.
Postcards a dollar. Knock-off Billy sombrero
with a Chinese dog skin vest? Ninety-nine bucks.
Oh, the turns of reckless, hungry youth, fame,
girls and borders, pistolero nights and cantina songs:
we live with deaf ears for the smell of gunpowder.

Happy Birthday, Gustav Klimt
(July 14, 1862 – February 6, 1918)

Today you are painting in your garden:
champagne-colored roses, edelweiss,
the voluptuous brunette model holding still,
yet in a languid attitude of availability…
alpine carnations, small sunflowers….

And two other girls are at-frolic in the garden,
the lithe brunette, a street nini, and escapee
from a parsonage or nunnery… who knows for sure?
And the new girl, a strawberry-blonde,
beautifully naked but for a blue leather
dog-collar-necklace… flame-red pubic hair…
spring bud nipples… her sweet voice
like raindrops on crystal goblets.

Your brush work is light, feather-soft.
The strawberry-blonde flirts,
asks if she would make
a wealthy young gentleman's cocotte,
floats past you in near-orgasm,
and you, you who dislike social life,
are aroused by intimacy with blush-radiant skin,
velvety skin. And the brunette you are painting
flows her hands down her breasts and belly
in joyful competition for your next caress.

Today, Gustav, at liberty, you are in your
fecund garden, painting a nude.
Science and industrialism enslave.
Eros, ecstasy-eternal, supple in gold
arousal-light, gives freedom.

Theodore Roosevelt   (1904)

He orders the train to a dead stop,
lumbers into high Nebraska blue stem grass.
In a hundred years, our luck must not
dog us. Beside Teddy, like forceps clamping
a stillborn's head, a Secret Service bodyguard
takes a fiddle from a bamboo case and sings
New York headlines. Summer thunder.
Teddy is on his way home to the White House,
braying love for his ranch on the Little Missouri.
We must not be strong-armed by knaves
who'd cut our timber to twirl velvet purses.
Porters spread a blanket among sun-whitened
bison bones and serve fresh roasted corn.
Teddy drinks from a shooting trophy mug.

Alfred Jarry's Toothpick

An iron gate shudders in the wind.
Behind a cottage, the bleating of goats.
A woman in a black veil passes by.
The cosmos of Alfred Jarry.

We are taking turns, Jarry and me,
riding his bicycle in the farmyard.
Jarry wants all information on contemporary
uses for simply constructed sawhorses.
He's sweaty from too much exertion,
confesses, *The last stranger I kissed*
was foaming at the lips… perhaps Tupsy.

On a short video from Jarry's backpack,
a diamond-glittery woman with a dancer's body
and lipsticked-black nipples
hand-mixes tomb ashes with perfume.

Jarry explains Munch, Rubescent clouds,
naked women, wild-desire frolics,
and the tardy arrival of texts
on assorted methods for bleeding the infirm.
Nicely marbled, finger-thick paper.

Three skinny coyotes stand mute and still
at a hundred yards range… watch Jarry
pedal in ever-smaller circles.
We also like the gentle opening of flowers,
the slow pulse the dead have achieved,
tomb-ebony river stones curated in tea cups.
Jarry tumbles in a tangle with his bicycle.
Muddy water flows from the handlebars.
He shrieks, *Merdre! Merdre! Merdre!*

Wyatt Earp   (1909)

The Mojave rattlers are terrified,
leave the old man to crawl copper holes.
He lists his occupation as *Mining Dynamo*
the winter of '09. *A man of sixty-one*
should not have to murder for Wells & Fargo,
but he shovels one more grave in the weeds
for a debtor to float below sand. Sadie huffs,
helps Earp lug a porcine-stink, heavy body
from their Packard's back seat, nags
that the car's brass trim is tarnished.
Midnight… it rains like ten men pissing.
Sadie slips into an unbutton-me-quick chaos dress,
but Earp is not in the mood. *Why,* she asks,
are we always one wretched mile from heaven?

Jack Johnson   (1909)

There is always time to gab.
The nice angle of having a white woman
is cheating on her. I love pea-green eyes.
Johnson thinks his end will come
in the sights of a rifle, not racing
a car into a tree. *I just can't stop*
eating padlocked peaches, he tells
Stanley *The Michigan Assassin* Ketchel
after their bout. Then it's lamb chops
at the Seal Rock Inn, poker and whores
in Colma. *When I think about God*,
Ketchel says, *it makes me cry.*
Nail holes never heal. Johnson grins,
Circle God to His left... unload a right.

Jack London   (1910)

Wind cuts through the manzanitas
like a last breath. London never knew
his father. He feeds tag-alongs
in Glen Ellenat his redwood table,
employs dozens to build and sail
the flawed Snark. Then the stone house
burns like folding money. He cuts a slice
from a chunk of plug tobacco, offers it
to Charian. *A writer is just a fellow
going bare knuckles against the ghost of God.*
He needs booze or a woman's legs twined
around him to get decent sleep.
I invented debt. He cannot choose
between Marx and Darwin: the wolf is alone.

for Johnny D. Boggs

Georgia O'Keefe   (1913)

Just above the too-hot weight of low Texas sky,
there are bone-white bones, a steer skull
with a kindly smile. Her Amarillo students
ask, *Why do you dress like a man?*
Alone, outside her rooms-by-the-week hotel,
she fights the impulse to dance the rhythm
of the wind. A trainload of cattle jerks
and groans eastward. *Why do I like to kiss
the boys, tongue and hard, but decline turnabout?*
And if the smoke from a lone cowboy's
campfire in Duro Canyon is golden-blackness,
heaven is a flower flattened between
textbook pages. *Loneliness is so lovely,
black vultures across Texas flat ground.*

　　　for Elizabeth Dear

Henry Starr   (1921)

He is driving to Harrison, Arkansas,
to hold-up a bank. It's not that far
from Tulsa if you're modern enough to quit horses.
He is forty-seven, four decades past holding
the reins of Cole Younger's gelding at Aunt Belle's.
This last time in prison cost him his wife,
the son, Teddy, named for Roosevelt.
Starr squints at his driver, *Normal life*
is the despair of cautious self-regard.
The carbuncle-faced driver blinks.
We won't get rich, the old outlaw says,
and we might not ever get to see home again.
Starr tilts his Stetson's brim over his eyes,
elated to be the last link to the James-Younger boys.

for Jimmy Butts

Warren G. Harding
(November 2, 1865 – August 2, 1923)

Bawl and sneer, he sets the curtains
so as to watch stolid cars on snow.
His heart clouts his spirit,
I'd be with her today
if I had some time back then.
He turns, silently watches
the latest hooker stumble
from the White House,
her open coat flapping crazy.
Harding kisses the label
of a half-full bottle of rye,
Love is pipe dream trouble.
The Oval Office is an ashtray
pimpled with booze bottles.
Harding lights a cigar,
calls for his night secretary.
Together they sing,
Sometimes baby hides
her sugar in a bank.

Happy Birthday, Sergei Yesenin
(September 21, 1895 – December 27, 1925)

The yellow-hued rope you hung yourself with
still swings in Moscow... back and forth, back and forth.
When Stalin got news, he danced in mockery of Isadora.

Five marriages in twelve years can wreck a man:
Anna was the first song of love, Zinaida sprinkled
lemon juice on the sheets, going-fat Isadora
gave you a taste of American bourbon,
and you hitched-up with Augusta before butter
could melt and soak into Isadora's rye bread toast.

Before there were movie stars, there were poets.
Perfumed silky girls, girls fresh from ten-chicken villages,
begged you to tease, to suck and love them...
more girls than all the wind-blown fir trees in Russia.
Vodka, vodka, more vodka... and more love:
Nadezhda Volpin gave you a poet son.
Near the break-furniture, set-fire-to-hotel-rooms end,
Sophia - Leo Tolstoy's granddaughter - dragged you
to a hospital for a no-vodka screaming month.

Now, on the other side, how do you, Jim Morrison,
and Georg Trakl, grind eternity? Do you run into Stalin?
Is there a heaven of peace? Is dinner promptly at six?
Do all five wives, and the hundreds of girlfriends,
offer sunrise kisses as you prepare to sleep all day long?

You might like it here, Sergei. Waffles for breakfast.
Dark tea. No smashed-head cadavers... like the ones
Stalin's thugs dragged you past to change your poetry.
Here it's quiet as the skittering of brittle autumn leaves.

Lyndon Baines Johnson   (1928)

Cadaver-thin, he stalks up the tracks
out of Cotulla, Texas. The tickle in his throat
gives way to the first whiskey in weeks.
Twenty, he is scarcely older than his seventh grade
Mexican students at Wellhaven Elementary School,
still blurts, too obviously oggles married women,
compulsively smokes, and damned well can't sleep.
At the edge of town, he bellows at the north wind,
My students will be stamped with learning,
will not be subdued. By God, they will cut loose,
immortal, and grow to love goodness, without hunger.
Then, in darkness, he mocks himself, says, *Shit.*
He winces at his own rhetoric, yet prays on his knees
to be sent on a terrible journey worth caring about.

for Larry D. Thomas

Happy Birthday, Kostas Karyotakis
(October 30, 1896 – July 20, 1928)

They placed no flowers on your dead man's bed.
The other poets of your time laughed at your
azure solitude, too stone-eared to know
your poems were the pain of the absolute-new.
Syphilitic, five-hour failure at drowning yourself,
you spent your last money on a rust-pocked pistol.
Your final poems were landlord-crumpled,
casual-tossed into a maggoty garbage bin.
You sang for skinny window-children
doubled-up in sorrow, for waste-away brides
waiting for war-maddened husbands,
for mothers bearing graveyard lilies.
You scribbled orange-moon poems by night,
you desire-stunted, pathetic, servile clerk,
you angel of rosy-marble cemetery aspiration.
From the corners of your glassy eyes,
you caught the half-hidden diamond-sparkle
in a farewell-scatter of oblivion-bound dirt.

Dante Benedetti   (1929)

It is dawn and the boy, mitt up,
flows through San Francisco morning fog,
sets himself near second base.
And Joe DiMaggio, a fisherman's son
at shortstop, pivots to throw.
Hard, hard, hard... growls Benedetti.
DiMaggio blazes a palm-stinger chest high
to start a double play. One will be a Yankee
and one will run his family's New Pisa Restaurant,
coach for two decades at University of San Francisco.
But this morning, three nuns fresh from Mass
smile and shout, *You got 'em*! And it goes on,
this practice, until Dante must go dice potatoes
white as brand new baseballs... for soup.

for Al Gallagher

Going to the Movies with Gertrude Stein

It is a bleak landscape and Gertrude is waving
fatty arms, spilling popcorn, laughing.
I am laughing, she says,
and a laugh is like a rash…
it spreads, which is what laughter does.

It is a desert that she sees on-screen
and, also, a wise old man who resembles
retinal consequence. Gertrude is laughing
at the wise old man's dingy look.
I have popcorn on my lap.
Gertrude is stuffed with popcorn.
Gertrude says that popcorn
is as American as fraud and Wall Street.

There are fumes in the theater
and they are coming from Gertrude.
Her stomach hurts. Her eyes are watery.
Gertrude tells me that she knows her stomach well.
A daughter is made to shut up and be sold,
Gertrude says, *like movies or a chunk of lard.*

Gertrude is not my type, no, and she is sweating,
her thick coat is soaked from a desert
thunderstorm we are watching on screen.
Gertrude says, *I do not care for the desert.*
The desert is truculent like a spindly widow.
A spindly widow is no less than brown sunlight,
but a brown sun is never truculent.

Outside the movie house, Gertrude
demonstrates what she calls *long looks.*
When we are looking, Gertrude says,
we are truly monstrous consequence.
Gertrude is making long looks.

Clara Bow (1930)

The hunger never eases and she cannot sleep,
nipples erect, Gilbert Roland and Gary Cooper
no more than the gleam of an ocean under stars.
The peachy satin sheet is cold and the red
ceramic tissue box is empty.
Here at the beach house, legs spread wide,
a suitcase mostly packed, she listens
to the leaky kitchen faucet, waits
for Rex Bell to phone her back.
He is up at Tahoe with Will Rogers
making another Western. She tries to sing
a cowboy song, but her voice is heavy,
river stones in a coat pocket.
The mirror trembles as she holds her breasts.

Will Rogers   (1935)

Think of bullhide boots left in the rain.
Or a lonely valley. Will Rogers loved speed.
Nothing quite matched riding *Soapsuds*
off a moving flatcar, getting it perfect
on the first take. There were other horses:
Dopey, Black Iron, and *Seven Squash.*
Think of a single engine plane
not gaining altitude over an Alaskan lake.
The abyss smells like burning rope.
Rogers made us laugh with the truth.
Think of an Eskimo boy running for help,
his shadow lit by aviation fuel flames
until there is no shadow, only the crackle
of a lariat snaring the northern sun.

for Johnnie Phillips

Joe, You Can't Talk to Me No More?

Before the two-year investigation,
before flat-foot ex-cops followed you,
saw you take an envelope from a race track hustler,
before being banned forever from baseball,
you, Julio Bonetti, sinkerball pitcher,
were a hero of Genoa, Italy…
only the 2nd Italian to make it to the Majors.

The DiMaggio brothers bought you
off-season San Francisco steaks,
cases of wine from Gino Benedetti's
New Pisa Restaurant in North Beach,
took you out on their fishing boats.
That was in-the-before… in the short years
men could do no better than weak grounders,
if you didn't walk those hitters first,
dribblers off a pitch that dove for diamond dirt.

Later, in the confessional with a snuff-breath
Irish priest down in San Mateo, you swore
you never did what they said you did,
throw a Pacific Coast League game,
Not for all the cash in Bank of Italy.
Later you hammered-up new homes,
crafted kitchen cabinets… *a Catholic
carpenter trying hard to please Jesus.*

Some Saturdays you'd drive for an hour,
past baseball parks where boys played
more fetch than catch. A nameless man,
you asked if you could throw batting practice.
No tricks, no velocity, you threw hitter-gifts…
then gave the kids the once-used baseballs.

You drove away, then, drove home weeping,
a man alone in a used Packard, a working man,
a specter old pals like Joe D. no longer saw.

Huron "Ted" Walters   (1938)

I never said I was some trigger-quick
matchless Lucky Luciano, Al Capone, or Dillinger.
You got to go a caliber extra in the crime shindig
to be a Clyde Barrow or Miss Bonnie Parker,
but you can tell folks I pitched pennies
with them. I have a talent for stealing
hens and eggs, for driving Cadillacs, and once rode
steers at rodeos as far north as Burwell, Nebraska.
I'm an ordinary, decent Texas boy, though my looks
are swank enough for Hollywood, wild sure,
but, until I met Clyde, my most daring adventure
was running around on Halloween, tipping over outhouses.
I'm in the Dallas jail thanks to Mr. Hoover… making me
Public Enemy Number One, your essential R.C. Cola thief.

Barbara Moffett   (1940)

A wolverine fur coat arrives in the mail.
California's Loveliest Showgirl tries it on
with black Nocona calf-high boots, nothing else.
On the radio, Wendell Wilkie says, *No more*
idle hands. We need two million new bathtubs,
millions of refrigerators, and no war in Europe.
At Hollywood's Florentine Gardens, Barbara Moffett,
ranch born and a champion roper at age twelve,
peels her jeans, peroxide blonde everywhere
pleasant, and five nights a week she puts on
a glossy slit-up-the-right-leg monkey skin dress…
and she strips… orchidaceous. But next spring,
road money earned, she hopes to win the Saugus Rodeo,
have a beer, go shirttail to the frisky wind.

for Mary Ann Bonjorni

Jinx Falkenburg (1941)

She does not wish to discuss the making
of *Song of the Buckaroo* or how they dyed
her mahogany-lustrous brown hair blonde
for a couple of *Lone Ranger* episodes.
I want more for Valentine's Day than a stale
this 'n that from a Whitman Sampler box.
At first sight of a camera, Jinx turns her head
so that only the right side can be shot.
I don't drink beer, but if I had to swallow something
so vile, I'd drink the brew that made me
The Rheingold girl. Jinx is in enamel bloom,
a shameless empire of beauty. The fellow who owns
all the sugar in Chile is at her Stork Club table,
holding her hand, offering snuff from a gold box.

    for Ciara

Jane Russell   (1941)

Between takes for *The Outlaw*, she buys round
after root beer round for the magazine pen-slicks,
says Howard Hughes does not have her nailed down.
Her square-jawed smile is as tough as saddle leather.
Someone gets Jane to chomp dried Hopi corn.
She gags, but swallows. *Sin is perishable,*
she laughs, *so you have to consume it quick.*
Old Tucson does not remind her of Van Nuys,
the high school boys who used to call her
Mona Lizard when she turned them down.
Is Ted Williams really that hot with his bat?
At the El Toro Saloon, Jane swaggers to the bar,
chest out. *Don't I look better in real life?*
Have a gander, boys, and pour on the roses.

for Chris Danowski

Happy Birthday, Cesare Pavese
(September 9, 1908 – August 27, 1950)

The sound of traffic on wet stones,
open summer windows, the smell of old boots
tossed against gray shrubbery… a young couple
passing arm in arm toward a lust-rippling bed.

And comes a picture of you alone with your pills…
your voice dead too soon… too-barbiturate-soon.
And your red clouds gargled lost love or decay
or both at the same time. You splintered soul.

And comes the sound of you walking past houses
scented with window box roses, bowls of peaches,
a woman's new black slip, dirty leaves in the pockets
of raw-muscled children… ungainly dreams.

There was no touching any love-glance moment,
was there, without taking a spear to the heart?

Gabby Hayes   (1951)

Shreds of plaid shirt, squares of felt Stetson,
clipped whiskers from his rough beard:
every fan letter deserves a reply, a gift.
Gabby rises at noon when not working,
laments the passage of love and intelligence.
He chooses a slim volume of Sapphic verse
from the nightstand, imagines skinny girls
on a Greek isle in the middle of the Mojave,
their feet roughened by spiny desert shrubs,
bellies hard as chimney brick. They are,
these blowsy-eyed angels, waiting for Gabby
somewhere outside Kingman. Gabby fills
each envelope with a keepsake, inserts
a small photo of himself as Agamemnon.

Dwight David Eisenhower   (1952)

Sign one for the wife, too, a man says
in Yuma, Colorado. Ike fleers at the poster,
his face in its toothy fever, eyes awash
with outrageous hope, like competing ovaries.
Running for President means shaking hands
with rum-breathed Bert Humney, pharmacist
to farmers, whose daughter ran off to California
after a tour with the Women's Land Army,
pickers of 1943's sweet corn. Now Ike
signs his name on the poster, black ink solid.
And Bert Humney, counter of capsules,
says, *I ain't hummin' when I tell you,*
General, when you're elected, it'll be time
to lock up those with weak nerves.

Hank Williams   (1952/1953)

They never tell you each road is a way
to meet shrill women who make you lonelier.
They never say the next train is short of seats.
When you bang your head on the inside of the back seat
car door, there's never a trim blonde angel there,
just the devil disguised as honky tonk radio music.
Morphined, chloraled, boozed: the snow
out on the highway is the color of watered down whiskey.
The last time you saw your star-wobbling soul in a mirror,
it groaned, *Every child is born to scare its momma.*
At least there's no factory grindstone, no Detroit
hotel room with a bare, blinding light bulb.
As two bottles clink on the floor below your jaw,
Hank, there ain't a way to turn around.

for Tom Russell

Happy Birthday, Stig Dagerman
(October 5, 1923 – November 4, 1954)

It's raining tonight… unsentimentally.
You did not wish for eternity.
Bent sunflower stalks bow to you.
Not exactly the outreached hand
that might have kept you with us.

The statistic is not handy:
how many sad men
walk each year into garages
and turn ignition switches
with no desert motel
to drive hard to…
just rev up the engine,
garage door shut,
and suck into their lungs
mankind's exhaustion?

Brother of the write-
a-poem-a-day compulsion,
you imagined more from others
than milk-hearted malice…
more from yourself
than confusion and weeping jags.

It was only a photo-op,
right, that portrait of you,
famed playwright, novelist of the bleak,
within a cluster of beautiful women?
Not the blessedness of love?
Did you wander out later
and embrace marble statues?

Happy Birthday, Leopold Staff
(November 4, 1878 – May 31, 1957)

All that glitter-love, when times were best,
was best ignored... just the shit-soiled
pajamas of the *Ubermensch.*

Silver cigarette case, wooden Franciscan crucifix,
half-starved children selling bathroom tile
lifted from bombed-out buildings.

An undulating purple dusk over Poland....
The cozy Marxist surfaces tarping brick rubble....
At least you sang on a chill evening.

Happy Birthday, Albert Camus
(November 7, 1913 – January 4, 1960

Tonight stars glitter on a two-lane blacktop,
a moment with no headlights… to remember your words.
Car window down, eyes watering, this high desert
night blows a pack's worth of Gauloises smoke at me.
Yes, it is best to live for the new and the superficial,
their divisions and the cobwebs that marry them.
Yes… no truths, only objects for love:
that tequila bottle, that girl with ice-silver eyes,
this rattling squirrel-dead road, that betrayed heart.
Caligula returns and returns and Caligula returns.
In this epoch, he who slays Caligula and his armies
is offered up as moron and left to the rain.
Long forgotten: the pair of Corinthian temples,
cheek to jowl, for Violence and for Necessity.
The stars are pearl earrings. The stars are
tiny onions. The stars are blood diamonds.
Yes, kicked doors, baffled priests,
lonesome hotels with freckled banana walls,
and executioners. Yes, absurd as it is,
I am looking for extreme experience in solitude.

Marilyn Monroe   (1960)

I don't have to wear a halo all the time.
She drooled like any chloral addict.
Waking up in her Mapes Hotel room's shower,
Marilyn asked for a steak sandwich,
skip the mayo. A make-up girl offered
to go find her a Paiute coyote fetish.
The gravediggers are waiting, Marilyn snapped.
Huston or Miller? She brushed her bone-blonde
dry-as-the-Great-Basin hair, concealed it
with a smoke-blue, flat brim Stetson,
announced that her ass was sore
from the pick-up truck in *The Misfits*.
She winked at Gable, *I used to remember*
all my lines when I was an angel.

for Kirk Robertson

Ernest Hemingway
(July 21, 1899 – July 2, 1961)

They puzzled you, James Joyce and Samuel Beckett…
their circular talk of one day seeing the Grand Canyon.
That was not your country, nor is the country I live in:
rock, sage, rattlesnake, rainless weeks and months.
It's precisely that broken and arid in the universities…
perhaps no change there: aged virgins prattling
against you, worry-eyed tweed men pleased
with their own self-battering. You never expected
to make friends in offices swollen with rancid custard.
Your words, still strong, most postmarked before my birth,
are tough to beat: you remain our Heavyweight Champ.
Trains no longer run on time, letters are email-bitched,
and the rich still announce forthcoming spousal splits
in expensive hotels surrounded by deep-green woods.
I imagine you forever homeward, a star we have
lonesome eyes on, permanent as your novels.

Happy Birthday, Johannes Bobrowski
(April 9, 1917 – September 2, 1965)

Johannes, we <u>do</u>, sooner or later
sleep each other's sleep. Like you,
I love villages at midnight…
or later as saloons empty
into the commotion of shadows.
After five years in one of Stalin's
coal mines, wrung-out every night,
head bowed to poems-in-progress,
you loved to gorge on marbled beef
from the pasture of mother Prussia,
pastries, sweet bread, shots of cream.
Was it a sharp, half-chewed nut
that broke your appendix…
forcing the journey across the river
to sleepwalk alongside Georg Trakl?
Young poets with rucksacks search
Germany for you in morning mist,
kids heavy with the imperative
of filling Moleskine notebooks
with scrape-by hikes along rivers.
We learn, eventually, at faint-last,
there is no *Here* to remain within,
no land of eternally full pantries.
Only the rivers remain…
older than poetry's first ink.

Happy Birthday, Kenneth Rexroth
(December 22, 1905 – June 6, 1982)

Blurry night over Japanese poetry…
girls on the scrounge for bread or love.
Later you open a used book shop
on San Francisco's Union Street,
make an easy dollar off review copies.
Ginsburg howls and steals your acolytes.
Marthe runs off with Creeley.
You dogpaddle into the deeper
ink-dark waters of haiku,
suffer academic parties
(lamp shades on skulls)
in Santa Barbara. Now the grave
facing the blue-green Pacific.
Small wonder that tonight
a couple of soft-belly
gloom-eyed poetry slammers
will spill wine over your words.

Happy Birthday, Charles Olson
(December 27, 1910 – January 10, 1970)

For some poets it's the cancerous clumpy liver.
For others it's blindness... tousles of white hair
from dewy-naked college girls with perky nipples.
That's for famous poets. Others get mildewed
cardboard to chew in shake-the-elderly rest homes.
Tell us again about Pound in St. Elizabeth's,
fire in his wired-tight eyes, leather restraints
when Ezra bellowed, gave the fascist salute,
America is a madhouse... shit-pouch of money lenders.
You beat a retreat. Well... several retreats...
rather unseemly for a big guy, right? But what the hell.
You had to write a great poem... one that could
snap in half the brittle, formal chair of poetry.
Golden buckets of strong drink to you!

Andrew Wyeth
(July 12, 1917 – January 16, 2009)

The apple-sweetness of desire,
enthrallment with a German girl,
someone else's wife. And, shy, you ask
if you might paint her. Borrowed attic,
autumnal field: Helga comes thirsty…
drinks plain iced tea from your tin cup.
You speak of distant stars or newspaper
delivery boys… only Helga in bed knows,
turning over and over, droplets of sweat
dampening an off-white Montgomery Ward's
cotton sheet. Her secret. Your secret.

Wild blonde hair, most often in pigtails,
no silly grins, her full breasts, farm-fit body
summer moist… she lets you,
rough-handedly, at first, position her
for the immortality of sugar-loaded light.
Wife untold. Husband untold.

Your hands skim perfect skin and you catch
the scent of oranges and leather gloves.
And she silently watches you bulge…
perhaps with a half smile and shrug.

In your last years, Helga strokes
your in-spasm muscles, props your head up
for an extra pillow, lets her hair down,
wild golden hair in light not tarnished
by fame for being your Helga…
muse and naked angel.

Happy Birthday, Norman Mailer
(January 31, 1923 – November 10, 2007)

Empty saloon, reddish neon light
shoots through thin, ink-smudged curtains:
even sloshed or stoned Mailer can shadow box
along the streets for miles… the sixties
Heavyweight Writing Champion of the World.
He keeps a lingering hard-on for Marilyn.

There is so much singing in Mailer's skull
that he speaks in a Texas gunslinger drawl.
He is in a sweat to write just one great
forbidden story… something musky
with raspberry breath, something dangerous
in the jungle of a whiskey-mad brain.

Mailer is in his prime as Kennedy is elected,
a lover of champagne pussy and mirrors.
He knows the heart of pugilistic increase,
how to take hope and bad fate into a ring
for fifteen bloody rounds, how to punch
fear and dread into the shadows
of our wretched, gone-plastic paradise.

Sonny Liston   (1970)

The silence is so sweet as Liston jabs a needle
into a log-size forearm. He is hardness,
quick hands, and he was the last time Ali was Clay.
Then *Night Train* bounces out of the record player,
lopes around the trophy room like a drunk dog.
I always wanted to say, "Love me,"
and I couldn't spit it out to no one.
Young fighters drop by after sparring
at Johnny Tocco's Gym, jump the prime rib spread.
His wife passes out napkins, *Sonny don't always be mean.*
Late morning is racing down Sunrise Mountain.
The desert is speckled with the bodies of men
who couldn't pay up. Liston shuffles, fists up,
to the curtains, peeks out, growls, *Boo*!

To the Memory of Ron Lyle

Ted Williams   (1972)

Dip the rear shoulder as you land
your front foot and you won't lunge
on a Wilbur Wood knuckler, goddamnit.
With his best Texas Ranger hitting .250,
manager Teddy Ballgame is tempted
to activate himself. He is fifty-four,
beefy, but how hard is it to sit back,
trust hips and hands, and drill Wood's pus?
Williams, 34-inch Louisville Slugger in hand,
swaggers to the water cooler. On defense,
his boys labor to field routine grounders.
If he was twenty years younger….
Williams shuts his eyes: Korea, 1953, his F-9
fighter is aflame in the closest game he'll win.

for Charlie Silvera

Waylon Jennings   (1974)

Guitar skitter 'n jump. It's a pounding bad-ass
surly song: Take your sorry chances,
'cause gloom is what we all deserve.
This is Pay-Later-Day, but if you can battle
past it, finally truth your way around cactus,
pretty baby will be there in a gold Cadillac:
Love. It's a Wednesday, probably, sweat and dread.
Waylon takes a pull off a cracked whiskey bottle,
can't sleep on the ebony Silver Eagle
somewhere between Chickasha and Mineral Wells.
It's a gambler's stew. Losers end at sixty
in furnished rooms… feeding D-Con to mice.
He laughs, jots down some lines on a girl
with a nest of vultures in her topaz eyes.

for Maura

Three-Fingered Dave Keefe
(January 9, 1897 – February 4, 1978

Lost the middle finger of your right hand
to a corn-cuttin' machine's blades
just weeks before taking your first steps?
No problem: you learn to grip a baseball
any way you can… invent the forkball,
strike out Babe Ruth three times in one game.

Your country goes to war, no problem.
You join the Navy. Baseball waits for you.
Major League hitters learn you're a one-pitch
trick pony. No problem: there's minor league
baseball in Milwaukee, Portland, Buffalo….

Too old to get minor leaguers out, no problem.
You talk to Connie Mack, become the first
professional Major League batting practice pitcher…
hittable enough to last twenty years to the delight
of Jimmy *The Beast* Foxx, Mickey Cochrane,
Al *Bucket Foot* Simmons… hittable enough.

For you, grandson of the Irish Famine,
Fermanagh blood in your Gaelic heart,
nothing is too difficult, no call to tough to answer.
Your hotel catches fire. You jog out at age eighty-one,
turn back at the cry of a fire-trapped woman,
pivot your still-hard body, run into the flames,
charge a flight of stairs, carry her down
to a Kansas City sidewalk… with a last smile.
There's a problem: smoky, ember-scorched lungs.

To the Memory of Joe Sprinz

Happy Birthday, Leo "The Lip" Durocher
(July 27, 1905 – October 7, 1991)

Gin rummy, poker, craps… great games
as long as you had them rigged, yet it was baseball
you held in rapacious, loving arms. In thuggish
boyhood, you stole money from Babe Ruth,
your roommate on the Yankees, then blackened
his eye for whining. Ruth called you, *The pimple
on this team's hairy fuckin' ass.* But Jackie
Robinson and Willie Mays bought your fatherly act.
You're buried somewhere in Forest Lawn,
Hollywood Hills Cemetery, near your pal
(and Bugsy Siegel's pal) George Raft.

Baseball, being a three-time Manager of the Year,
got you the friends you loved to name drop,
just as Frank Sinatra and Dean Martin dropped
your name. Sparse hair expensively dyed wine-red,
blue eyes on fire, you blurted, *Nice guys finish last.*

At the end, too stove-up for swank golf
at the Tamarask Country Club in Palm Springs….
In the extra innings, your cranky eighties,
the beautiful women vanished, you hedged bets,
prayed to Jesus… with a con man's wink.

Elvis Presley
(January 8, 1935 – August 16, 1977)

At the slack and blubbery end,
Elvis could no longer shake it.
It was dumb sleep, harsh daylight
outside, curtains drawn, stone-blue pills,
the arms of a couple of local girls
across his soft, barely rising and falling
gluttony-ruined chest. The girls
were left awake as *The King*
dreamed schoolyards and Jesus hymns.
I'm gonna be his next pretty wife,
one girl would say to the other.
They'd pillow fight over the top
of his girdled *Viva Las Vegas* belly.
The King would gasp for breath,
a torn pillow's goose feathers
tickling his nostrils and plump lips.
One of the girls would kiss him,
brag, *His eyes glaze at the lovely*
sight of my smile, then tap the diaper
changed every eight hours by men
with gold *TCB* medallions and rings.
The last girl awake knew what to say,
what to pity-please into his ear,
Oh, daddy, I'm yours forever.

Happy Birthday, Vladimir Holan
(September 16, 1905 – March 31, 1980)

Swindled by Marxists, euchred by popes,
you thought an evening with Hamlet could
glisten-up tarnished nights. Solitary mornings…
afternoons of unbuttered rye bread and tea,
rides on random elevators to nod at impossible
milk-white breasts, impartial crimson lips.
At last, overwhelmed by the stench of piss
racing in their veins, you gave up corresponding
with foul-wind Shakespearean scholars.
How goes it in the abyss, Vladimir?
Little better, I suppose, than month upon year
in your Kampa Island apartment by the tomb-
dark waters of the Devil's Stream… center of Prague.
I am with you tonight… your sober-waltz poems.
Leninist and Papish cunts: it was a harmony of lies,
stone-grins, bad wine from pus-crusted shoes…
a horror broken every so often with what is human:
fresh hope like summer light off silvery pewter.

Happy Birthday, Eugenio Montale
(October 12, 1896 – September 12, 1981)

Loud quarrels, shoppers, gripes:
Milan with a red billboard
in blue evening rain…
a street of squared gray stone,
luminous rail tracks,
a web of overhead wires,
couples in love… and the lonely.

Perhaps God listens to gossip.
Perhaps the premise for the divine
is thin barley soup, no cubed lamb.
Every paradise I entered was crowded.
Sugary kisses in Aspen,
blueberry scones in Sun Valley.
The brittle flow of walkers
gave off the sound of ice
splitting basalt. Like you,
I tried to locate the *Good*.
Knowing the final result is carbon.

Let us drink, Eugenio Montale,
gloom-poet, poet of golden lines
at raw solitude-hours.
Let us sing invisible songs
of autumnal storm-dream…
majestic confections of eternity.
What gain from collapse-pensive
or doubt? It is no time to envy the dead.
But my clumsy hand reaches out to you.

Andre Breton's Nadja... in San Francisco

Rather than appear for her audition
at the theater on Geary, she sends a wine cork.
There is moral value in presentation.

Nights alone at the Gaylord Hotel:
Breton's ghost flaps along hallways…
his red concrete blanket turns to powder.

The stamp collector in room 314 shouts,
Who gave me this paisley bellyache?
Nadja toasts him with raspberry vodka.

Nevertheless, it is Bastille Day among electric
palaces up on Pacific Heights, in the homes
of staved-in, intoxicated diplomats.

And Nadja feels tardy. She begins a letter,
*Dearest Andre, if I did not appear affectionate,
my map to joy was cigarette-burned at its folds….*

Long-legged Nadja strolls naked across
the Golden Gate Bridge… the ocean westward
no more to her than weed-green curtains.

I am a chilly river, she sings, *caught
behind a movie screen… Clark Gable roping
wild horses as Marilyn Monroe smolders.*

Nadja is in San Francisco with Dominican nuns
-Mission San Jose- now crowding her every step,
so she hides in her room, drinks more vodka.

There is cheering from the street below her room.
It is Bastille Day and granite-eyed Andre is falling
one silent raindrop at a time from a perfumed cloud.

A Dirge for Paul Funge
(1944 – 2011)

It was an exaltation of pure joy… the painting,
the friendships near and windblown.
Now it's better to laugh, stifle a growl…
better to remember us drunk in San Francisco,
a short walk to the surf, snug and well fed
in a surviving '06 quake Victorian,
bombastic for art and poetry…
four decades ago… how you passed out
on a wide couch in a bottle-clogged
front room, my Irish Wolfhound, Bran,
curled at your feet, proprietary guard
of your sleep, your dreams of new paintings.

How could we have known that afternoon
in Gorey, Wexford, us in our twenties,
when James Liddy walked me through
your new festival, when you talked, joked
a verse-wilted sweet-nippled girl
into my arms, anointing me,
The new crazy-great Yank poet…
how could we have known, in that Gaelic sun,
that the nicotine-yellow fish-scale-fleshed
Abaddon of the Bottomless Pit
would stalk us, trip us into the icy
trap of lights-out codgerhood?

All these decades… no words between us.
My fault the silence. Wheeling onward with poems.
Giving sweet Kate babies. Never gathering wit
long enough to at least send you a postcard.
Tonight it's not nearly enough to grieve-stare
at your paintings, luminous on a techno-screen.

Yet that is what your friends must get by on:
the luminous work, paintings you gave with joy.

Postcard to Kay Boyle

Dear Kay, The Revolution never arrived.
Tonight, far off, flames are singing
to a black sky, a Gaelic god's
shameless indifference. The half-inspired
novelist-revolutionaries you fed
on Frederick Street are now seventy,
glum in Tenderloin hotels stacked with tales
no one will publish. A few have chucked words
to craft strawberry-scented candles
on the Mendocino coast… and their meth-addled
children hate the patchouli stench of them.
I hope you have forgiven me for using
your letter of introduction to Beckett
to light a turf fire in Donegal. Kate bakes
brownies as if our kids are still home.
I spend nights walking toward a fire
maybe twenty miles across this high desert.
God love you, Kay. Never slack-jawed,
never too weary to insist on marzipan
for every living soul, you were beautiful
as soft Irish rain. Where you are,
I hope you have settled in with your beloveds,
Joyce, McAlmon, Beckett, and Ernest Walsh…
and that Hemingway is not
there to taunt you.   Love, Red

After a Dream of Hollywood Ponies

Majestic, slow movie music fades into the miles...
toward a paint-flaking, old and empty, stock tank.
The man cannot see horses from his window.
Daylight... rain clouds: memory of raspberry kisses.

Two-thousand years of scruffy mornings ago
the emperor Trajan, to celebrate a birthday,
had wolf hides tied to glass-eyed Christians...
set beautifully muscled Irish Wolfhounds upon them.

Oh, the rapture of long-gone champagne kisses.
A moist-browed woman shuffles a hotel's
desert-hot hallway... a small plastic tub of ice
for morning-swollen, hard-lessoned eyelids.

And the emperor Trajan settles his god-body
where Nerva, Domitian, and the others sat battle-proud.
Fifty-thousand lip-foamy Romans, nobility and rabble,
stand and cheer man's fate: blood-euphoria.

Dead faces melt, form again in dark-pewter clouds.
Sleeping lovers cling to one another in a surrender
turned to comet dust. A Hollywood film pony
carries a cold stranger through a whistling canyon.

Hunter S. Thompson
(July 18, 1937 – February 20, 2005)

The management does not believe you're dead,
not at San Francisco's, far-from-downtown, Seal Rock Inn.
There's a suite reserved for you… stocked
with Wild Turkey, a mountain of grapefruits,
a sack of Peruvian coke, and the desk clerk
is doing all he can, with pepper spray,
to disperse over a dozen *friends* with quick-printed
invites to your party. They are sure the doctor is in…
that the good times are triggered to roll. You'd recognize
the ocean-view room. You trashed it, trashed it again…
and management declared it *The Gonzo Suite.*
Among friends shooting Silly String at the desk clerk
is Riya, owner of a Tenderloin massage parlor.
Riya says, *I'm fifty-three goin' on nineteen.*
You'd recognize this, good doctor, as a humble-tussle,
only the weird-grief of story makers, autobiographical
fantasists who perhaps, in better and wilder days,
shook your hand, perhaps read *Songs of the Doomed*
to children as bedtime stories. At peak, San Francisco
will be 64-degrees by late afternoon, cloudy… wonderful
for a roar down the Great Highway and then south
on 280 to Woodside where pot is still queen,
where shrines to you are constructed
with redwood burl, slight effigies of Hubert Humphrey…
targets to be shot dead-dead-dead…
because you might have led the festivities.

More... Your Gunslinger Shadow Grows Amber

To observe (absorb?) the enduring dead...

(Mysterious Dave Mather dead and wormy
in an Oakland flophouse
suggests the late work of a civilized West...
and no mystery beyond a need-of-cleaning
pistol mentioned in the crumbly will.)

... you must allow yourself
to be a lone figure
{clouds like concrete pressing down}
breaking your interior (ceiling?) calling.

All that aged, rotted flophouse drywall
falling in chunks from the heaven of others.

Old pal Bat Masterson yet approaches
his squarish New York City journalist form.
Steak-clogged arteries.

These are primary juxtapositions:
Old West and walking pantomime.
What a goddamned trick:
levitation with the dead.

To the Memory of Ed Dorn

About Red Shuttleworth

Poet and playwright, Red Shuttleworth is the author of *Western Settings* (University of Nevada Press), *Johnny Ringo* (Riverhouse Lit), and over thirty poetry chapbooks, including *We Drove All Night* (Finishing Line Press). He is the recipient of two Spur Awards for poetry from Western Writers of America and *True West* magazine named him "Best Living Western Poet" in 2007. Shuttleworth's poems have appeared in over 200 literary journals, including *Los Angeles Review, Ontario Review, Prairie Schooner, South Dakota Review,* and *Weber: The Contemporary West.*

Shuttleworth's play *High Plains Fandango*, which takes on the prospective privatization of water, of aquifers, premiered at State University of New York at Fredonia in early 2012.

Over two-dozen of Shuttleworth's other plays have been presented widely, including at the Foothill Theatre (CA), Sundance Playwrights Lab, Sun Valley Festival of New Western Drama, University of Nebraska at Kearney, and the Tony Award-winning Utah Shakespearean Festival.

www.ingramcontent.com/pod-product-compliance
Lightning Source LLC
Chambersburg PA
CBHW071423040426
42445CB00012BA/1275